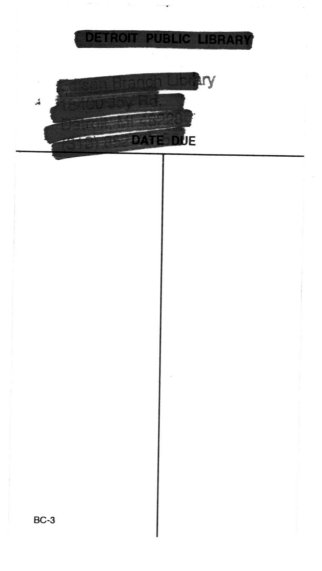

A Day With A
Maya

A Maya

by Federico Navarrete Linares

Illustrations by Andrés Sánchez de Tagle
Translated by Laura Dulin

Runestone Press/Minneapolis
A Division of Lerner Publishing Group

All words that appear in **bold** are explained in the glossary that starts on page 43.

This edition first published in the United States in 2000 by Runestone Press

Runestone Press
A Division of Lerner Publishing Group
241 First Avenue North
Minneapolis, MN 55401 U.S.A.
Website: www.lernerbooks.com

Consejo Nacional Para La Cultura Y Las Arts, Dirección General De Publicacions, Mexico (Andrés Sánchez de Tagle): 13 (bottom),9 (bottom), 11 (right). Mercedes De La Garza, Mexico: 13 (left). Davide Domenici, Milan: 10 (right), 14 (top left). Editoriale Jaca Book, Milan (Stefano Martinelli): 9 (top); (Antonio Molino): 13 (right); (Angelo Stabin) 8 (top); (Cristina Tralli):10 (bottom), 12, 15 (bottom), Mireille Vautier, Paris: 10 (top left), 14 (bottom left). Drawings by Merle Greene Robertson, in Merle Greene Robertson, *The Sculpture of Palenque*, Princeton, Princeton University Press, 1983-86, v. 2 *The Early Buildings of the Palace and the Wall Paintings*, fig. 91, fig. 73.: 11 (left), 14 (right). Drawing by Diane Griffiths Peck, in Michael D. Coe, *The Maya*, London, Thames and Hudson, 1987, p. 169: 15 (top).

Library of Congress Cataloging-in-Publication Data

Navarrete Linares, Federico.
A Maya / by Federico Navarrete Linares; illustrations by Andrés Sánchez de Tagle, translated by Laura Dulin.
p. cm. — (Day with)
Simultaneously published in English and Spanish.
Includes bibliographical references and index.
Half title: Day with a Maya.
ISBN 0-8225-1922-4 (lib. bdg. : alk. paper)
1. Palenque Site (Mexico)—Juvenile literature. 2. Maya artists—Mexico—Palenque (Chiapas)—Juvenile literature. 3. Maya pottery—Mexico—Palenque (Chiapas)—Juvenile literature. 4. Mayas—Social life and customs—Juvenile literature. 5. Palenque (Chiapas, Mexico)—Social life and customs—Juvenile literature. I. Sánchez de Tagle, Andrés. II. Title. III. Title: Day with a Maya. IV: Series.
F1435.1.P2N38   1999
972'75016—dc21   99-17214

Manufactured in the United States of America
1 2 3 4 5 6 - JR - 05 04 03 02 01 00

CONTENTS

INTRODUCTION

More than 10,000 years ago, bands of hunter-gatherers crossed a land bridge that then linked Asia to North America. By 7000 B.C. **Mesoamerica**—the area that would become Mexico, Guatemala, Belize, Honduras, and El Salvador—was home to hunter-gatherer societies. Mesoamerica extended into the deserts of northwestern Mexico. But most of the region was dense with vegetation. Pine forests covered highlands and mountains. Rain forests blanketed the warmer, wetter lowland areas, dominated by huge **ceiba** trees that stood as high as 150 feet and created a dense **canopy.** Thick jungles, broad savannas and humid swamps also patched the lowland landscape.

People settled in small villages and began to practice agriculture. The Mesoamericans grew corn, beans, squash, and other foods. Deer, turkey, and rabbits provided wild game. Over time different languages, cultures, and religions arose. Crocodiles, jaguars, and poisonous snakes—animals of the region that posed dangers to humans—played roles in the mythology of many Mesoamerican cultures. The different cultures believed that human actions, such as sacrifices or proper behavior, could influence the actions of the gods.

Followers of these different cultures traded artifacts, ideas, and raw materials. Seashells from coastal areas and **obsidian** from the highlands traveled across Mesoamerica. Some villages grew from trade or religious centers into massive city-states. Skilled artisans made the cities beautiful, and talented farmers raised enough food to feed urban populations. But wars also broke out. Some were fought between rival cities of a single culture. Other wars erupted when different cultures vied for control of a region.

The Mayan civilization flowered in the Classic Mayan period (A.D. 300–900). Workers built huge stone cities. People developed sophisticated farming techniques and a **hieroglyphic** writing system. The study of astronomy and mathematics led the Classic Maya to create a highly accurate calendar. Skilled artists painted murals, carved stone, and made beautiful pottery. Farmers carved fields out of swamps.

Series Editors

PART ONE

THE WORLD OF THE MAYA

On Mexico's Yucatán Peninsula, the homes (above) of modern-day Maya are similar to the straw and earth dwellings of the Classic Maya (below). The Classic Maya arranged their houses around courtyards.

Huge temples and palaces dominated ancient Palenque (facing page, top). During the Classic Mayan period, more than 100 cities dotted Mexico, Guatemala, Belize, and Honduras (facing page, below, and inset).

Classic Mayan civilization was marked by the rise of huge city-states on the Yucatán Peninsula. Thousands of Maya lived in and around Palenque, a city in what would become the state of Chiapas, Mexico. Powerful royal rulers, called **ahau,** governed the cities and the surrounding farmland.

Jungle, rain forest, and wet swamps surrounded Palenque, which was in the tropical, lowland area of the Yucatán Peninsula. Workers cut away dense vegetation to create space for the farms, the canals, and the city buildings of Palenque. The splendid Palace of Palenque was home to the ahau, who lived surrounded by courtiers, jesters, priests, and musicians. But most Maya were artisans or farmers who lived in small, one-room houses. They mixed mud with straw to build walls, and they roofed their homes using thatched palm leaves. Several houses usually faced a courtyard. People slept indoors, but most cooking, eating, and socializing took place in courtyards.

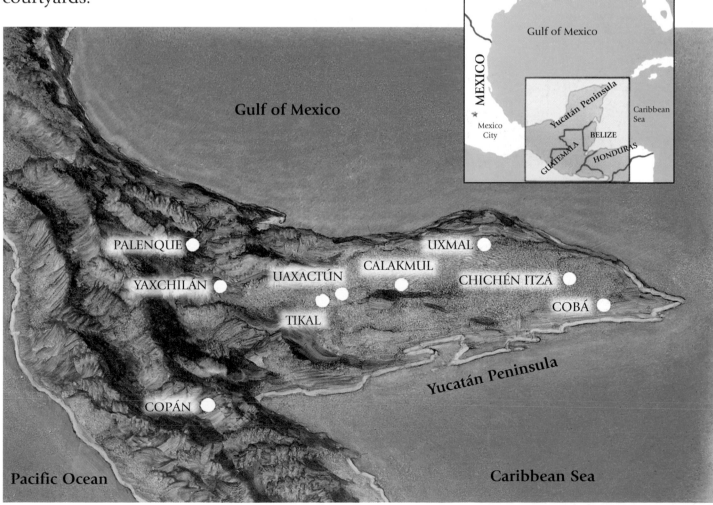

Farmers raised corn, cotton, squash, chili peppers, and beans. They cut away at hillsides to make smooth, terraced fields. They turned swamps into fertile farmland. Workers dug a network of deep canals through the swamps to create small islands. The farmers spread the muck from the canal bottoms on the islands, making them into fields. And when the canals began to fill with silt, the workers dug them out again. Between February and May—the hottest, driest time of year—Mayan farmers prepared their fields. If the rainy season didn't begin at the end of May, the year's crops might fail. Then the Maya could go hungry.

Classic Mayan farmers spent part of the year building massive, limestone structures like the **Temple** of the Foliated Cross and the Palace of Palenque. Workers quarried limestone slabs, transported them to the building site, set the slabs in place, and mortared them together. A thick coat of plaster gave the buildings a smooth surface.

The Maya believed in many gods. Sacrifices—especially of human blood—persuaded gods to help people. Blood may have been

The Temple of the Foliated Cross (above) *in Palenque, constructed for* **Chan Bahlum**. *The city developed around the temples and the Palace of Palenque* (above, left), *where the ahau lived in great splendor, surrounded by servants, musicians, dancers, and jesters. This stucco head represents Chan Bahlum* (facing page, top). *Pacal received signs of power from his mother, Zac Kuk* (facing page, bottom). *Zac Kuk was the ahau before Pacal, who was Chan Bahlum's father.*

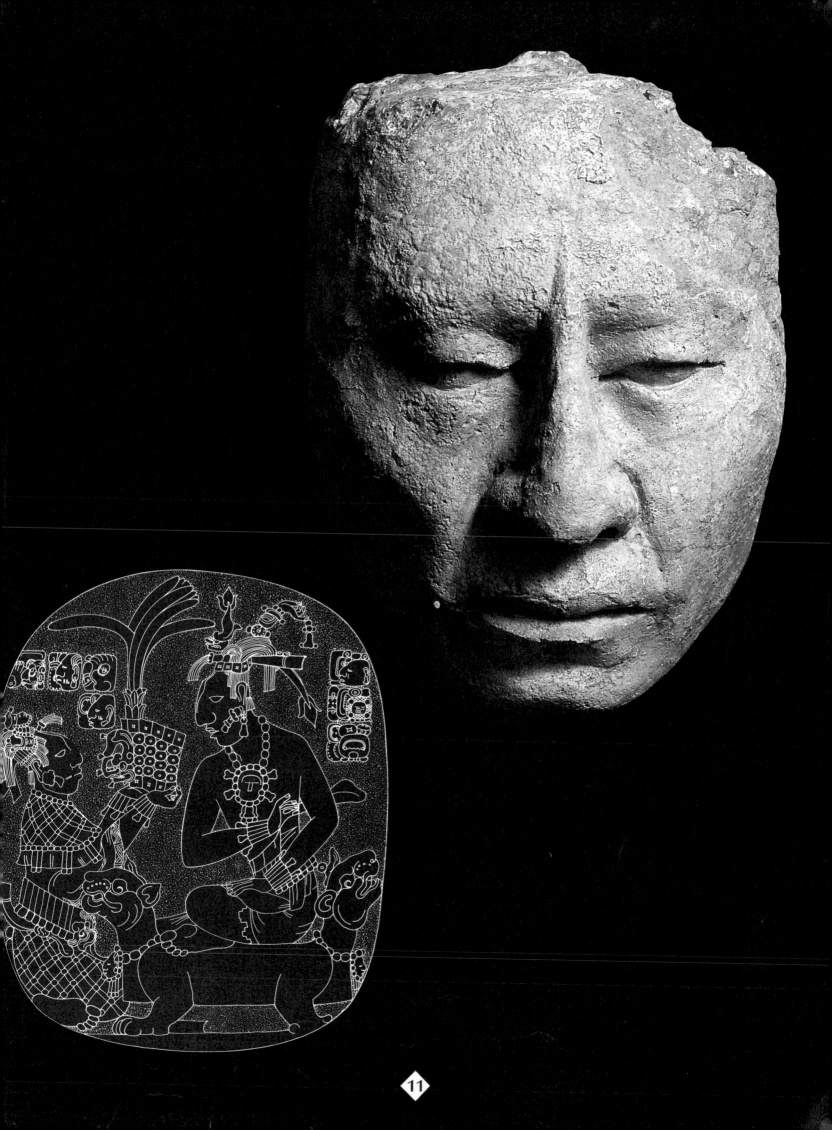

The twins Hun Batz and Hun Chuen, gods of letters and of the arts, paint a vase.

considered food for the gods. The Maya may have believed that blood opened a pathway between earth, heaven, and hell. People probably marked occasions such as birth, marriage, and the burial of the dead with bloodletting rituals.

The Maya of Palenque believed that an ancestor of their ahau had been a god. Therefore, the ahau linked the Maya to their gods. The ahau tried to protect ordinary Maya from droughts, diseases, and other disasters, which were the cruelty and punishment of the gods. Rulers sacrificed their blood to influence gods at crucial times, such as when the community needed rain.

Priests probably organized Mayan religious practices. The priests might have also been astronomers and mathematicians who used math to plan annual events, such as the harvest. They perfected the accurate Maya calendar.

The Maya believed that highly skilled artisans (called *itz'at*) could create objects with souls that guarded the ahau's sacred powers. This power was dangerous for the itz'at, whom the gods could help or hurt. Classic Mayan artisans mastered many skills, including complex painting on ceramic pottery, on rock, on bones, and on wood. They also worked at carving, sculpture, and writing using hieroglyphs. Artisans crafted **codices** (books) from **leather** and a clothlike paper made from bark or hide. In codices and in carvings, artisans recorded Mayan mythology and information about rulers and wars.

Two gods—the twins **Hun Batz** and **Hun Chuen**—inspired the artists. According to Mayan belief, these gods of letters and arts tried to kill their younger brothers, the hero twins Hunahpú and Ixbalanqué. As punishment, the gods were transformed into **howler monkeys.** But Hun Batz and Hun Chuen remembered their knowledge and continued to protect the arts and writing.

According to Mayan belief, souls were immortal. Above the earth rose thirteen layers of heaven, supported in four corners by four ceiba trees. Below the earth lay nine underworlds, each ruled by its own god. The god of death, Hun Camé, ruled over the other gods. He lived in Xibalbá, the lowest underworld. The center of the universe was a ceiba with branches in the heavens and roots in the underworld. This tree—Great Mother Ceiba—linked the heavens, the earth, and the underworld.

The Maya buried their rulers in magnificent tombs. In Palenque's Temple of Inscriptions, the ahau Pacal's body was placed in a 25–ton sarcophagus carved from one massive stone. Engravings of Pacal, his ancestors, and his successor Chan Bahlum covered the sides and lid. A narrow passage led from the tomb to the temple's inner chamber, which allowed Pacal's soul to influence the living.

During religious ceremonies, worshipers burned incense (scented tree gum) in this large, colorful vase (left). This clay head may be a portrait of a Mayan noble (above).

Pacal's stone coffin (above, top) was shut by a five-ton stone slab. An engraving on the lid showed Pacal descending through Great Mother Ceiba to the underworld (above, left). Pacal was buried wearing a funeral mask made of jade, a semi-precious stone (above, right).

(Facing page, top) *Six gods of the underworld sit in front of Hun Camé. Above him a crocodile, which symbolizes the earth, shows that this scene takes place in the underworld.* (Facing page, bottom) *Hun Camé is shown as a skeleton.*

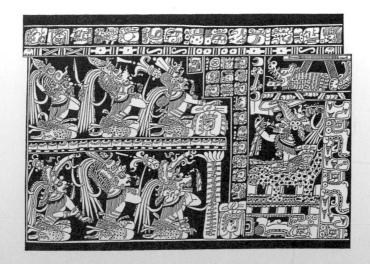

Xibalbá, The World Of The Dead

According to Classic Mayan belief, the spirits of the dead Maya lived in Xibalbá. Hun Camé ruled Xibalbá with the help of the lords of death, who dwelled in temples and palaces. Around them were the ordinary Mayan dead, who suffered illnesses and accidents at the hands of the cruel lords of death.

The Maya believed that long before the creation of the world, the hero twins Hunahpú and Ixbalanqué had visited Xibalbá, where they were killed by the lords of death. The twins were resurrected, and they killed the lords of death in turn. Knowing a way to overcome death, the hero twins taught humans how to travel from Xibalbá to the House of the Ancestors in the Heaven of Dawn.

The Maya buried their dead with food, drink, and many objects. They also buried the dead with beautiful objects to give to the gods. The dead used these gifts to bribe Hun Camé to let them pass through Xibalbá to the Heaven of Dawn. There the dead were believed to guard their living relatives and to send them rain and prosperity.

The Classic Mayan period ended about a thousand years ago. People left Palenque, as well as many other cities in the region, at about that time. But modern-day people know a great deal about Classic Mayan life. By examining **artifacts, archaeologists** discover what materials and techniques the Maya used. Human remains reveal to scientists what sicknesses the Maya had and how long most people lived. By studying graves, specialists learn about how the Maya viewed death. Some experts have deduced trade routes by figuring out which artifacts came from distant sites. Aerial photographs show that the swamps were once made into raised fields. Terraced fields retain their shape, too.

Although codices and carvings remain, the Maya ceased to use their ancient writing system. For hundreds of years, no one knew how to read the hieroglyphs on Mayan art and buildings. In the 1950s, scholars figured out the meanings of many of the symbols. Experts could then decode inscriptions to learn about Classic Mayan rulers, wars, and religious practices.

Anthropologists study aspects of modern-day Mayan cultures. For example, Mayan speakers use more than 20 dialects, so maybe the ancient Maya did, too. Another way to learn about the Classic Maya is to figure out the challenges they faced. For example, because the Maya were farmers, they must have been concerned about their crops getting the proper amount of rain.

All of this information can be carefully pieced together to create a detailed image of what Mayan life was probably like. Let's travel to a morning in late May of the year A.D. 702.

PART TWO

A DAY WITH KAWIL, A MAYAN ARTIST

Even before sunrise, the day was hot. **Kawil** woke up dripping with sweat. From his hammock, he saw a fire on the hearth. His mother was already preparing **tortillas.** Kawil ran to the courtyard to cool himself off outdoors, but there, too, the air felt burning hot. The rising sun had painted the treetops of the ceibas red. He saw the temples shining white and the jungle's thick green foliage. The *guacamayas* and the howler monkeys seemed to greet him with their calls. The sky was cloudless, and the dry earth fell through his fingers like sand. Kawil heard a grave voice sing out near him.

"Today the sun, the Guacamaya of Red Fire, can burn the entire world. Palenque could catch fire and we could all burn to death."

Kawil stood up and saw an old man wearing a spectacular headdress with orange feathers. He carried a death's head medallion on a long wooden pole. Kawil recognized the supreme priest of Palenque.

"O great leader! It is an honor that you visit this humble artisan," Kawil stammered.

"Yesterday our ahau, Chan Bahlum, died," the priest announced sadly.

"Without our king, there is no one to bring the rain. Without the rain, we won't be able to plant the corn. We all will die of heat and hunger," Kawil said, fear invading his entire body. The ahau was the only person who could intercede with the gods.

Together the priest and Kawil entered the one-room house. Near the door was a long table loaded with vases and jars that Kawil had painted. In a corner, Kawil's mother prepared a tortilla on the **comal.** His brothers sat near her, already eating. The sour, penetrating smell of the **nixtamal** filled the house. Kawil's mother handed him a fresh tortilla, but the priest took it.

"No, Kawil—you must fast to show honor to our ahau," said the priest. "Today you will paint a vase to be entombed with Chan Bahlum, who will carry it to Xibalbá as a gift to Hun Camé. The vase must be so beautiful that the god of death loves it. Then Hun Camé will permit Chan Bahlum to cross Xibalbá. Our ahau will arrive at the Heaven of Dawn and send us rain."

"But I'm not an itz'at! I can't paint a vase with a soul. I'm just a regular artisan," responded Kawil, his voice trembling. The priest gazed at the young man and then looked at the rows of jars that Kawil had painted.

"You are most highly skilled, Kawil. But if you fail, your vase will be an insult to Hun Camé. He will not let our ahau pass. The rain won't come, and the people of Palenque will die from thirst. And you will be the first to die."

"The vase must be ready at sunset, and already the sun rises," said the priest, and he walked along the road leading to the city. Kawil's mother quickly embraced her son.

He followed the priest to the Temple of Inscriptions. At the top was a tiny temple, bright and hot. Above an altar, torches lit a relief of the gods Hun Batz and Hun Chuen. Near it Kawil saw a plate loaded with strips of paper. The priest knelt before the relief and handed Kawil a long, thin spike made of obsidian.

"Use this holy needle to call Hun Batz and Hun Chuen," the priest said. "They will guide you."

Kawil watched the priest slowly walk back down the side of the temple.

Kawil sat in the small temple. He couldn't hear the cries of the howler monkeys in the forest. Kawil breathed deeply. He set the plate piled with strips of paper in front of him. Then he took the obsidian spike and, with a single movement, pierced his tongue. He slowly pulled the needle all the way through his tongue. His hot blood sprinkled the paper in the bowl.

His eyes were tightly shut and his breath was rasping when the needle finally slid from his tongue. He prayed to the twin gods until his voice sounded strange. He opened his eyes and saw that blood had soaked the paper, so he took a torch from next to the altar. It was difficult to set the damp, red heap on fire but finally it sizzled. Black smoke filled the sweltering temple. If the gods were not pleased with him, they would kill him. He felt dizzy but heard howler monkeys calling out as if from a great distance.

"Come with us, itz'at," they seemed to say, "Come and learn how to paint the holy vase." But then Kawil realized that he was fainting.

Opening his eyes to the bright mid-morning sun, Kawil was glad to be alive—but he was in a shady hut deep in the jungle. The priest must have ordered him carried here. Two howler monkeys sat down on a large bag made of jaguar hide. Kawil greeted the monkeys, which shouted before scrambling back into the jungle.

Kawil opened the bag and found the tools he would need—a length of snakeskin, some paintbrushes, a jar of black ink made from soot, a shell in which to mix paints, and jars of pigments.

He dipped a paintbrush with stiff fiber bristles into the black ink and drew a border on the snakeskin. Then he outlined the area for the dedication, which could give the vase a soul.

He paused, brush in hand, and felt that he could never create a picture worthy of Hun Camé. Kawil shut his eyes, trying to relax. Peace crept over him as he listened to the monkeys calling, the birds singing, and the foliage rustling. He opened his eyes. When he drew, his hand moved as if it had a will of its own.

It was noon when Kawil finished drawing the outline. He felt weak and hungry. His tongue was painful. But he was satisfied with the image. A sudden movement caught his eye, and he saw Balam, the best potter in Palenque, standing at the clearing's edge. The man approached the hut with his head bowed.

"Itz'at! Excuse me, but I bring two vases. You must choose which one to paint. I made them when the priest told me our ahau was dying."

Kawil felt proud but nervous when Balam addressed him with such respect. Kawil took the vases and sat down to examine them. One was straight, and the other was rounded. They were light, with sides so thin that Kawil could have snapped them apart. Both were perfect.

"These vases are the best that my stupid hands could do, itz'at!" explained Balam, and Kawil almost laughed at the thought of the potter being clumsy.

"Sacred twins Hun Batz and Hun Chuen! I hope that I have chosen correctly!" Kawil said. He gave the round pot back to Balam, who vanished into the brush.

In a moment, the great priest appeared from the forest. Kawil handed the snakeskin to the old man, who examined it.

In the image, Chan Bahlum emerged from a huge snail shell that floated down a river crossing Xibalbá. In front of him Hun Camé held a knife with an obsidian blade. The god of death could use this knife to kill the soul of Chan Bahlum. But Chan Bahlum carried the gift of a vase.

"This is the work of a true itz'at," said the priest, "You are only missing the dedication."

Kawil sat down to draw the symbols in the space he had left, surprised by the strength of his hand.

"On the day of the death of Ahau Chan Bahlum, this vase was created and blessed. May the ahau drink **chocolate** with Hun Camé, ahau of Xibalbá," read the priest when Kawil had finished. "You are missing something very important." The old man smiled at Kawil's startled expression.

"What is it?" he asked.

"Your name," the priest said kindly.

"But my name is not dignified enough to appear on a sacred vase," the young man stammered.

The priest, already walking back into the jungle, did not answer.

Kawil sat down and arranged the tools very slowly. The brushes were perfect and the pallet had been made from a beautiful shell. These sacred objects had been used by itz'at of Palenque many times.

Kawil shut his eyes and took a deep breath. The jungle seemed silent. He wondered if the twin gods had decided not to help him. Then he placed the vase on a wooden stand and began to paint.

First he picked up the fine brush and outlined the designs of the borders. The most difficult part was drawing the blood river of Xibalbá. Kawil took the vase in his left hand, turning it slowly as he painted the curves of the river and the snail shell. Last he drew the figures of the ahau holding his gift and of the god Hun Camé clutching his knife.

The sun was in the western part of the sky when he finished outlining the scene. The next part was easier, but it still required great skill and steady hands. Kawil took a brush with firm bristles and painted the background yellow. For the red color of the blood river of Xibalbá, he pricked his ears and mixed his blood with the pigment. Finally, he used blacks, browns, and reds to paint the elegant profile of Chan Bahlum and the sinister figure of Hun Camé.

Before painting the dedication, Kawil breathed deeply. Then he took a stiff, narrow brush. With thick black paint, he traced the complex figures that formed the words. To finish, he very carefully wrote his name: the itz'at Kawil.

The instant that Kawil set down the vase, Balam the potter came from where he had been waiting in the forest. He took the vase, careful not to touch the wet paint. He would fire it in his kiln. When the potter left, Kawil lay down, exhausted, and fell asleep. He thought he heard the calls of howler monkeys. But he realized that Balam was trying to wake him.

"Itz'at, get up! You have to carry this holy gift to the tomb of Chan Bahlum! It is late—the sun is sinking toward Xibalbá," the potter said, holding the finished vase.

Kawil rose and examined the work. He felt the warmth of the kiln in the clay, but the colors had become brilliant. It was more beautiful than he had hoped it could be.

The sky was an orange haze as Balam and Kawil walked to Palenque. Kawil felt hungry and his tongue throbbed. Monkeys were shrieking into the darkening jungle. He dared not guess if they were mocking or guiding him.

Soon Balam and Kawil saw the city's temples and passed people who called out, "Run, itz'at! The sun is setting!"

Clutching the vase, Kawil sped along the path and through the crowded plaza. He dashed up the steps of the pyramid to find the priest waiting.

"Hun Camé will surely admire this," the priest said, looking at the vase. "Hurry now! Our ahau will leave us at sunset, which opens the door to Xibalbá."

The old man handed back the vase, and he showed Kawil a staircase that led down to the heart of the pyramid. Kawil descended until he reached three masons closing the tomb's entrance with blocks of stone.

Torches of perfumed wood lit the tomb. Kawil passed beautiful skins, feathers, and bowls of fruit, **cacao** beans, and honey. Near the ahau's thin, stiff body, he remembered that ahau had loved music so much that Palenque's best musicians had always played near him. Kawil felt sad that the ruler would never hear their music again.

Then Kawil saw the bodies. The musicians had been sacrificed to accompany the ahau to Xibalbá. Kawil heard rocks moving into place. His pity turned to terror. Perhaps the priest would send him to the kingdom of the dead as well! Trembling, Kawil put the vase on the floor and ran toward the door. Then he stopped. He was an itz'at. The future of the ahau and of Palenque depended on him. He went back, picked up the vase, and filled it with cacao beans from a bowl.

"Take this gift, oh great ahau! May it be so beautiful that it enchants your enemy, Hun Camé!" he said, placing the vase in Chan Bahlum's hands.

The temple walls still echoed with his words when the priest's voice boomed.

"Leave this place, itz'at! We must close the tomb!"

Kawil crawled through the hole and watched the masons set the last block in place. He left the pyramid quickly, fearing that Hun Camé disliked the vase. But in the plaza, his mother greeted him with a smile.

"You are an itz'at!" she said as she pointed to large red and black clouds racing across the sky. Thunder crashed, lightning flared, and rain poured down. Hun Camé had approved the gift. Chan Bahlum had sent rain to keep Palenque from drought and famine. And Kawil had helped.

The crowd shouted and laughed with joy. They praised their ahau for the gift of rain. Kawil gave thanks to Hun Batz and Hun Chuen. Soon he would find Balam to congratulate the potter on his share of the work. But now Kawil celebrated.

AFTERWORD

After the death of Chan Bahlum, his brother Kan Xul ruled Palenque. But the Classic Mayan age began to decline within a century. Fewer buildings were constructed, trade decreased, and the population shrank. Finally, Palenque and many other Classic Mayan city-states were deserted.

A combination of problems probably led to the city-states' collapse. Powerful rulers may have become tyrants who lost the support of their subjects. Wars may have disrupted trade and weakened the power of the city-states. Famine, disease, and hardship could have led people to leave their homes in search of new and better lives.

Many Maya settled in other cities on and around the Yucatán Peninsula. Some cities, such as Chichén Itzá, became new centers of trade and religion. Strong links with other Mesoamerican cultures, particularly that of the Toltecs, led to new ideas in art and building, but records were still kept in codices.

In the 1500s, Spanish explorers arrived and swiftly conquered the Maya. Many Maya died from diseases unknowingly brought by the newcomers. Missionaries arrived to convert the Maya to Christianity. The missionaries burned hundreds of codices and outlawed Mayan religious practices, but the Maya preserved their beliefs. The Maya worked hard laying roads, building churches, and laboring on huge plantations for little or no money.

When Mexico won independence from Spain in 1821, the Maya hoped that times would improve. Government promises were broken, so in 1847 the Maya of the Yucatán began to fight for freedom from Mexico. Called the Caste War, the struggle lasted until 1901, when Mexico defeated the Maya. But in 1937, the Mexican government turned many plantations into small farms for the Maya. Some Maya chose to live and work in towns and cities.

These days between 2 million and 5 million Maya live across Mexico, Belize, Guatemala, and Honduras. Many follow religions like the faith that Kawil knew. They use the traditional Mayan calendar and live in houses like Kawil's—but many have cement walls or tin roofs. Despite many changes, the Maya preserve aspects of their unique culture.

GLOSSARY

ahau: A Mayan word for royal rulers who governed Mayan city-states. The ahau succeeded a parent—usually a father—in ruling the city-states.

archaeologist: A scientist who studies the material remains of past human life.

artifact: An item crafted by a human.

cacao: A tree that produces a fruit, the seeds of which are known as cacao beans. In Mesoamerica cacao beans were very valuable.

canopy: The high level of a forest, primarily made up of topmost tree branches.

ceiba: A large tree found in tropical rain forests in America.

chocolate: A beverage made from cacao beans, chilies, and honey.

codex: A Maya book, often in the form of scrolls or strips of paper. Maya writers recorded information that was very important to them, such as myths, astronomy, and genealogies.

comal: A clay disk on which tortillas are cooked over an open fire.

Chan Bahlum: This ahau of Palenque ruled from A.D. 684 to 702. During Chan Bahlum's reign, the Temple of the Cross, the Temple of the Foliated Cross, and the Temple of the Sun were constructed. His name means Jaguar Serpent.

guacamaya: A rain forest bird related to a parrot. The Maya considered the birds to be manifestations of the sun god, called the Guacamaya of Red Fire.

hieroglyphic: A system of writing using picture symbols to represent concepts and sounds.

Some Mayan artists painted vases with scenes of palace life. The ahau, seated on the right, receives two nobles and a servant carrying gifts. Two courtiers bear torches.

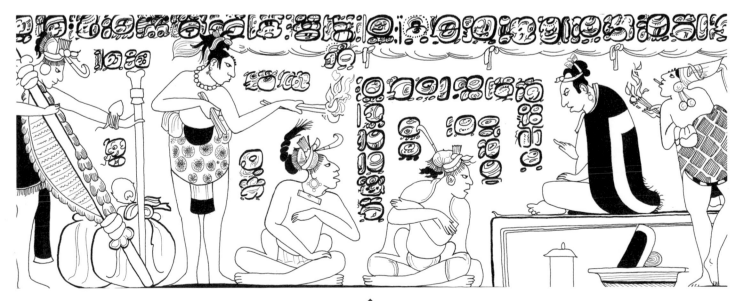

howler monkey: A small monkey with a long tail. The monkey makes loud, howling noises.

Hun Batz and **Hun Chuen:** Twin gods of writing, painting, and the arts. They take the form of howler monkeys.

Kawil: The name of the Mayan god of blood.

leather: The Maya highly valued the hides of jaguars, deer, and other animals of the tropical rain forest. They used these hides to decorate their rooms and furniture.

Mesoamerica: An area that includes modern-day Honduras, Belize, Guatemala, and much of Mexico.

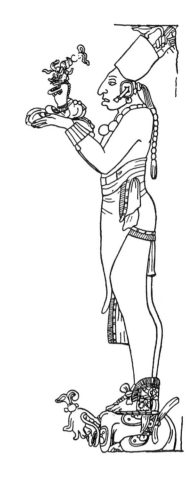

This portrait of Chan Bahlum comes from a panel at the Temple of the Sun in Palenque.

The Maya depicted the god Kawil as having one foot—or sometimes, one leg—in the form of a snake.

nixtamal: A mixture of finely ground cornmeal and lime used to make tortillas.

obsidian: Volcanic glass that can be black, gray, or dark green in color. It was used to make needles, knives, and other sharp objects.

temple: A large, pyramid-shaped stone structure. Here the Maya kept the images of the gods. Tombs of kings were deep within some temples.

tortilla: A thin, round bread made from nixtamal. Tortillas are often rolled up around meat or beans.

PRONUNCIATION GUIDE

Balam	bah-LAHM
ceiba	SAY-bah
Chan Bahlum	CHAHN bah-LOOM
Chichén Itzá	chee-CHEHN eet-SAH
comal	coh-MAHL
guacamayas	wah-cah-MAH-yahs
Hun Batz	HOON BATZ
Hun Chuen	HOON CHWAYN
itz'at	EETS AHT
Ixbalanqué	eesh-bah-lahn-KAY
Kawil	kah-WEEL
Kan Xul	KAHN SHOOL
Maya	MY-ah
nixtamal	neesh-tah-MAHL
Pacal	pah-KAHL
Palenque	pah-lehn-KAY
Xibalbá	shee-bahl-BAH

FURTHER READING

Baquedano, Elizabeth. *Aztec, Inca & Maya.* New York: Knopf, 1993.

Chrisp, Peter. *The Maya.* New York: Thomson Learning, 1994.

Galvin, Irene Flum. *The Ancient Maya.* New York: Marshall Cavendish, 1997.

Green, Jacqueline D. *The Maya.* New York: Franklin Watts, 1992.

Mexico. Visual Geography Series. Minneapolis: Lerner Publications Company, 1998.

Nicholson, Robert. *The Maya: Journey into Civilization.* New York: Chelsea House, 1994.

Sherrow, Victoria. *Maya Indians.* New York: Chelsea House, 1994.

Trout, Lawana Hooper. *The Maya.* New York: Chelsea House, 1993.

INDEX

About the
Author and the Illustrator

Federico Navarrete Linares was born in Mexico City in 1964. He earned a degree in history from the Universidad Nacional Autónoma de México (UNAM) and a master's degree in anthropology from the London School of Economics. He is an investigator at the Institute of Historical Investigations at UNAM. Also a professor on the Facultad de Filosofía y Letras at UNAM and at the Escuela Nacional de Antropología e Historia, he has given conferences at institutions in Mexico and abroad.

Andrés Sánchez de Tagle was born in 1956 in Mexico City and studied at the Escuela de Artes Plásticas at the Universidad de Guanajuato, Mexico. He helped restore paintings by the artists Cabrera, Echave, and Herrera in the Regina Coeli Chapel of Mexico City. In 1981 he worked on the restoration of 20 works by Baroque painters, including Villalpando, Cabrera, and Herrera. Between 1987 and 1989, he had three personal art showings in Mexico City. For the Economic Culture Fund of Mexico City, he illustrated the series Historias de México.